# THE HORTEN FLYING WING
## IN WORLD WAR II

Göttingen: Left Walter, right Reimar Horten. In the background the H II (left) and H IIIb (right).

## The History & Development of the Ho 229

# H.P. Dabrowski

*Translated from the German by David Johnston*

**Schiffer Military/Aviation History**
**Atglen, PA**

## SOURCES:

R. Horten/ P.F. Selinger: "Nurflügel", Graz 1983
D. Myhra: "Horten 229" Monogram Close-Up No. 12, Boylston 1983
B. Lange: "Typenhandbuch der deutschen Luftfahrttechnik", Koblenz 1986
T-2 Report "German Flying Wings Designed by Horten Brothers", Wright-Patterson AFB 1946
W. Rösler: "Bericht über den Fluganfall des Turbinen-Nurflügel-Flugzeuges Horten IX, V2.. ." (1985, unpublished)
Working Discussion on the 229 Mock-up (13. 10. 1944)

DVL Short Report on the Testing of the Flying Characteristics of the Horten IX V-1 (Berlin-Adlershof, July 7, 1944)
Power Plant Installation in Go 229 (Horten), (V3+V5), March 7, 1945, Junkers Flugzeug- und Motorenwerke A.G.
Flight Log of Lt. Erwin Ziller via Dr. Jörg Ziller
Correspondence with W. Horten, R. Horten, H.J. Meier, D. Myhra, K. Nickel, W. Radinger, R. Roeser, W. Rösler, H. Scheidhauer, P.F. Selinger, G. Sengfelder, R. Stadler.

H IX V1 is towed into its hangar at Oranienburg in the summer of 1944 following a test flight.

## PHOTOGRAPHS:

W. Horten
R. Horten and H. Scheidhauer via P.F. Selinger
W. Radinger
D. Myhra
P. Petrick

M. Griehl
H.J. Nowarra
B. Lange
W. Rösler
G. Sengfelder
F. Trenkle

Published by Schiffer Publishing, Ltd.
77 Lower Valley Road
Atglen, PA 19310
Please write for a free catalog.
This book may be purchased from the publisher.
Please include $2.95 postage.
Try your bookstore first.

We are interested in hearing from authors with book ideas on related subjects.

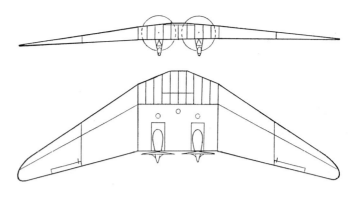

## The Horten 229 Fighter-Bomber
## The Horten H V, H VII and
## H IX All-Wing Aircraft

### PRELIMINARY REMARKS

The subject of "all-wing" aircraft is too extensive to be covered in depth here. Therefore, only the Horten H V, H VII and H IX (the latter also known as the Ho or Go 229) will be dealt with, all of which were twin-engined aircraft.

Doctor Reimar Horten, together with Dipl.Ing. Peter Selinger, has written about all of his aircraft in detail in the book *Nurflügel* (Weishaupt Verlag, Graz 1983). Major Walter Horten, at that time Technical Advisor of the General of Fighters in the *Reichsluftfahrtministerium* (RLM), made feasible the realization of his brother's designs.

Drawing of the H Va — the forward view approximates the aircraft sitting on the ground. Below: The H Va under construction. The stress bearing material used was the synthetic Trolitax.

### NOTHING NEW UNDER THE SUN . . .

When the newest American super-bomber, the Northrop B-2, was revealed to the public at Palmdale, California on November 22, 1988, many aviation history enthusiasts must have noted that the configuration selected by the aircraft's designers, namely that of the "flying wing," had been resurrected from the dead, as it were. Although present day experience has shown that the all-wing configuration is the best one for avoiding detection by enemy radar (aided by the

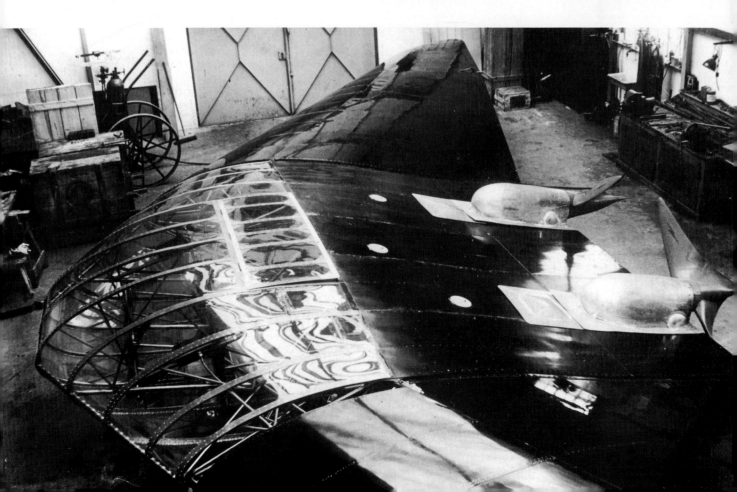

The crew of the H Va occupied prone positions with their feet forward, and as a result the aircraft did not have a conventional canopy. Below: Comparison with a motorized H II.

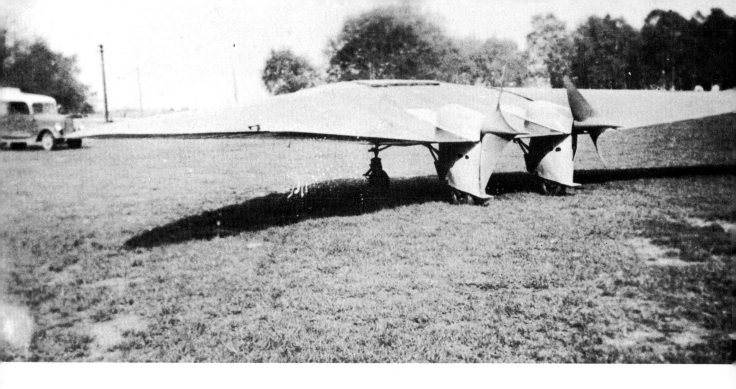

The H Va ready to fly. Noteworthy is the unusual shape of the aircraft's propellers. Produced by Peter Küpel, the propellers were driven directly, without extension shafts.

latest technology in materials, electronics and computers), the same configuration has been in practical use since about 1930. The first jet-powered all-wing aircraft flew in Germany on February 2, 1945, and at the time was also virtually undetectable by radar, partly on account of its mixed construction (wooden wings).

In the United States, John Knudsen Northrop had been working on all-wing aircraft since the end of the 1920s. His first aircraft of this con-figuration (although it did employ two small vertical tail fins on thin tail booms) was the "Flying Wing," which flew in 1929. Because of poor economic conditions during the 1930s, Northrop's twin-engined all-wing N1M did not appear until 1940, and the N9M until 1942.

Individual projects were undertaken in various countries, but in the Soviet Union there were numerous attempts, some of them very promising, to learn the secrets of the all-wing aircraft. The most successful Soviet designer was Boris Ivan-ovich Chernanovski, who developed a series of projects from 1921 to 1940.

In Germany, the Horten brothers, Reimar and Walter, had in mind a pure all-wing aircraft with no vertical control surfaces of any kind. Inspired by the Stork- and Delta-type tailless aircraft of Alexander Lippisch, they began their work at the end of the 1920s. Successful flight tests of their first tailless glider were carried out at Bonn-Hangelar airfield in July 1933. By 1934 they were working at Germany's "Gliding Mecca," the Wasserkuppe. The all-wing concept had achieved its first practical success.

Although development of the all-wing aircraft began at about the same time in Germany, the Soviet Union and America, there was no col-laboration whatsoever between designers. In spite of this, design teams in these widely-separated parts of the world were convinced that the all-wing aircraft was the best configuration and pursued the idea with much idealism. It is no wonder, therefore, that the concept has been revived in the present day.

The Northrop "Flying Wings" and the twin-engined Horten H V, H VII and H IX aircraft described herein can in a way be considered the forerunners of the B-2.

The H V was a pure research aircraft equipped with two counter-rotating pusher propellers. The H IX was designed as a twin-engined, turbojet fighter-bomber, and the H VII, also with two pusher propellers, was intended to serve as a trainer for jet aircraft. Detailed descriptions of the three types follow.

### Horten V a, W.-Nr. 5

The H Va was built in 1936/37 in cooperation with the Dynamit AG in Troisdorf, near Cologne. A synthetic material (Trolitax) were used in the aircraft's construction. Use of this material resulted in a series of problems, even though the glider *Hol's der Teufel* had previously been built using this method. Several of the solutions to these problems were patented by the Dynamit company. The nose of the H V was covered in clear Cellon, and the two pilots occupied prone positions. The aircraft was fitted with a tricycle undercarriage with faired main members (only the nosewheel was retractable), and the two Hirth HM-60-R engines drove two-bladed pusher propellers directly (no extension shafts). The propeller manufacturer Peter Kümpel produced the propel-lers from Lignofol (beech wood impregnated with synthetic resin). The H Va introduced novel movable wingtip control surfaces.

The H Va following its crash: as a result of the brittle nature of the synthetic material the aircraft was completely destroyed; only the aircraft's engines survived relatively intact.

The aircraft's only flight took place at Bonn-Hangelar in early 1937. In the aircraft were Walter and Reimar Horten. The extreme aft location of the engines made the aircraft unstable, and at its low takeoff speed the aircraft's controls were unable to overcome the resulting tail-heaviness at the moment of rotation. The H Va became airborne briefly, then crashed, damaging the aircraft seriously. The injuries sustained by the two men were relatively minor (Walter Horten knocked out his two upper front teeth). Following the accident the Dynamit AG collected the remains of the H Va to carry out tests on the materials used in its construction.

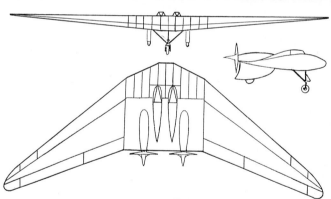

Three-view drawing of the H Vb, seen above while under construction at Cologne-Ostheim. The photographs below illustrate the excellent view from the cockpit afforded the aircraft's crew. In contrast to the H Va, the crew of the H Vb were accommodated in conventional seated positions.

The H Vb ready for takeoff; below: the aircraft with landing flaps extended.

Below:
Cologne 1937: the propeller shape has been changed from that of the H Va.

### Horten V b, W-Nr. 9

The H Vb was a research aircraft built at Cologne-Ostheim using conventional construction methods (wood and steel tube) on instructions from Major Dinort with the approval of Ernst Udet. As a result of the accident with the H Va, the movable wingtip controls were dispensed with and the designers turned to more conventional elevons. The Hirth engines of the unlucky H Va were used again, but were positioned further forward and drove their propellers via short extension shafts, resulting in a more favorable weight distribution. The H Vb's pilots sat upright next to each other and were provided with individual raised canopies. Like the H Va, the H Vb had a fixed tricycle undercarriage. The aircraft's

The aircraft seen from ahead with landing flaps extended, and ready for takeoff at Cologne-Ostheim (below).

first flight took place at Cologne-Ostheim in autumn 1937 with Walter Horten at the controls. From the beginning of the war in 1939 until 1941 the aircraft was parked in the open at Potsdam-Werder airfield, which was not altogether beneficial for an aircraft built largely of wood.

*Horten V c, W.-Nr. 27*
**Efforts by the *Luftwaffe-Inspektion* 3 (Lln 3, or Luftwaffe Inspectorate for Fighters, whose Technical Department Head was Walter Horten) succeeded in convincing *Generalflugzeugmeister* Ernst Udet that it was advisable to return the H V to flying status. In August 1941 a special detachment of Lln 3 was formed in Minden to oversee the reconstruction of the aircraft by the Peschke Firm.**

Below:
Side view of the H Vb, which was built using conventional materials.

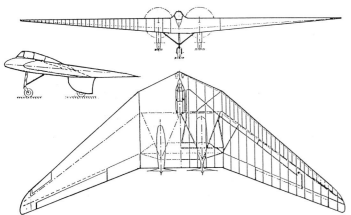

A three-view drawing of the H Vc. The series of photographs on this page depict the Peschke-built aircraft at Minden. In the photo, above left, is Otto Peschke (extreme left), seen while being shown an H IV glider.

The photo on the right provides an idea of the relative sizes of the H Vc (left) and the H IV. In the photo below, Walter Horten is seen examining the recently completed aircraft.

The photograph on the following page shows Walter Horten climbing into the cockpit of this aircraft. Visible is the forward-folding hood, as well as the window on the underside of the aircraft which provided the pilot with a downward view.

Peschke, a former WW I fighter pilot, had established a flying school at Hangelar and later an aircraft repair facility at Minden. The latter facility repaired aircraft such as the Fw 44 *Stieglitz*, He 72 *Kadett*, Fi 156 *Storch* and the RK *Schwalbe*. Peschke and the Horten brothers knew each other from Hangelar. In charge of the Lln 3 detachment was Luftwaffe *Leutnant* Reimar Horten. His team consisted of three designing engineers and five other men, including Heinz Scheidhauer, an experienced all-wing glider specialist. Later the special detachment was moved to Göttingen and enlarged to thirty men (soldiers, engineers, craftsmen and so on).

The Horten Vc was converted from the H V b, which had been badly damaged by the elements. In Minden the two-seat H Vb became a single-seat aircraft. The pilot was accommodated in a normal seated position. The H Va's Hirth engines were retained, as were its steel tube and wood construction and fixed undercarriage. As property of the military, it was finished in standard Luftwaffe camouflage and was assigned the code PE + HO (PE for Peschke and HO for Horten).

The H Vc made its first flight on May 26, 1942. Walter Horten later flew the machine to Göttingen, where *Luftwaffenkommando IX* was being formed.

*Flugkapitän* Prof. Dr. Josef Stüper, then Director of the *Instituts für Forschungsflugbetrieb und Flugwesen* (Institute for Flight Research and Aviation) at the *Aerodynamischen Versuchsanstalt (AVA) Göttingen* (Göttingen Aerodynamic Research Institute), carried out test flights in the H Vc. Late in the summer of 1943 an incident occurred involving the H Vc. Stüper took

Above: The H Vc in flight over the Göttingen area. Below: The aircraft lands in the evening twilight.

The Horten Vc in flight. The photograph below provides a view of the underside of the aircraft, revealing the military code PE+HO. PE stood for Peschke and HO for Horten — the RLM raised no objections to the use of this combination.

*Flugkapitän* Prof. Dr. Josef Stüper of the Göttingen Aerodynamic Research Institute was involved in a crash in the H Vc. The airfield fire-fighters doused the aircraft with foam as a precautionary measure.

The aircraft was certainly damaged in the crash, but not so badly that it could not have been rebuilt.

The professor (center) inspects "his" crash. He wears an unhappy expression, which is not surprising in view of the circumstances surrounding the accident.

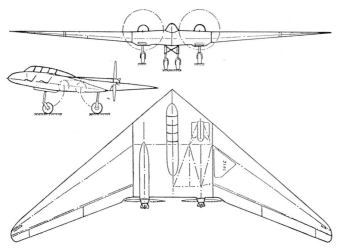

Left: A three-view drawing of the H VII, and above an artist's concept of the aircraft, drawn before construction began. The aircraft in the drawing features pointed propeller spinners, similar to those used by the H Va.

off from the center of the airfield with the aircraft's flaps in the down position. The aircraft's undercarriage struck the roof of a hangar and the H Vc crashed. Stüper escaped without serious injury, but the aircraft was badly damaged. It was subsequently stored at Göttingen in anticipation of restoration following the end of the war. Events were to prove differently, however, as all of the aircraft held there were assembled at the edge of the airfield and burned following Germany's surrender. A projected glider tug based on the H Vc was not built.

### Horten VII, W.-Nr. 29

Construction of the H VII took place at the Göttingen Bureau. The aircraft's wings, which were of wooden construction, were built by the Lln 3 workshop, while the center section, which was of welded tube steel construction with Dural skinning, was manufactured by the Peschke Firm in Minden. The aircraft made its first flight in May 1943 with Heinz Scheidhauer and Walter Horten on board. The aircraft had originally been conceived as a flying test-bed for the Argus-Schmidt pulse-jet engine after the H V had proved

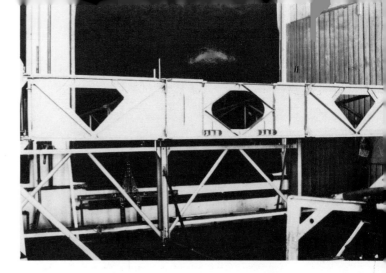

unsuitable for the role. When this plan was abandoned it was proposed as a fighter training aircraft. The H VII was powered by two Argus AS-10-C engines driving two-bladed constant-speed propellers via extension shafts. The aircraft featured a fully retractable twin nosewheel undercarriage. So-called "wingtip rudders" were used in place of a conventional rudder. The aircraft was assigned the RLM-Number 8-226. The aircraft's pilots were Heinz Scheidhauer, Erwin Ziller and Walter Horten. In autumn 1944 *Oberst* Knemeyer demonstrated the H VII to Hermann Göring at Oranienburg, after the *Reichsmarschall* had expressed a desire to see a Horten aircraft in action.

Knemeyer was the RLM flight-test chief and was favorably disposed toward the aircraft developed by the Horten brothers. Göring, a former WW I fighter pilot, had not participated in the later gliding boom and was unfamiliar with the aircraft which emerged from the program. He wanted to see the aircraft fly on one engine, which

The photographs on this page depict the H VII V2, which was largely similar to the V1, while under construction. The two photographs, below right, show the starboard wingtip rudder in the extended and retracted positions, while the one below shows one of the aircraft's engines with cowling removed. Visible are the extension shaft and the propeller brake.

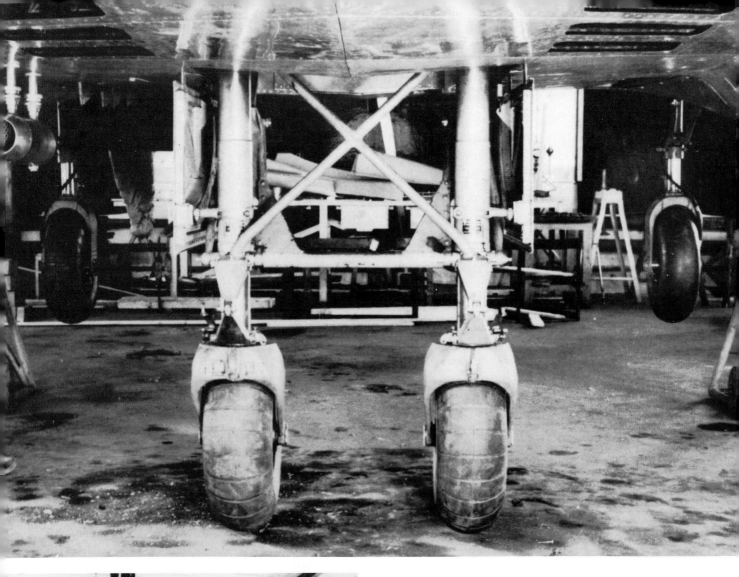

Details of the H VII: Above, the retractable twin nosewheel undercarriage; below left, the starboard propeller with automatic pitch control; below right, one of the aircraft's landing flaps, which were of metal construction, in the extended position.

Right: The wing of the H VII V3 under construction — the V3 dispensed with the so-called "wingtip rudders." Below: The H VII V1 in final assembly. The V1 was the only aircraft of the H VII series to be completed and flown.

Heinz Scheidhauer did without any hesitation. The *Reichsmarschall* was impressed; the Peschke Firm received an order for twenty examples.

Construction of the H VII V2 began in 1944, but the aircraft had not been completed when the war ended. The V3, which was to see the "wingtip rudders" replaced by spoilers above and below the wings, as on the H IX, progressed no farther than the manufacturing of various components.

In February 1945 Heinz Scheidhauer flew the H VII to Göttingen. Hydraulic failure prevented him from extending the aircraft's undercarriage, and he was forced to make a belly landing. The resulting damage had not been repaired when, on April 7, 1945, US troops occupied the airfield. The aircraft presumably suffered the same fate as the H V and was burned.

### Horten IX V1, W.-Nr. 38

Walter Horten was aware of the performance achieved by the DFS 194 rocket-powered research aircraft, and thus knew that wooden construction methods were suitable for high-performance aircraft. After seeing the Me 262 in March 1943 he set out to acquire information on the Jumo 004 turbojet engine. Further work on the H VII was abandoned and all efforts were concentrated on the H IX, which originated from Göring's 1000x1000x1000 demand, in which the *Reichsmarschall* specified that no new project would be considered unless it achieved the following performance figures: a speed of at least 1,000 kph and the ability to carry a 1,000 kg bomb load 1,000 km into enemy territory. Justifiable deviations from these figures would be accepted. At that time

Stress tests being carried out on the H VII V1.

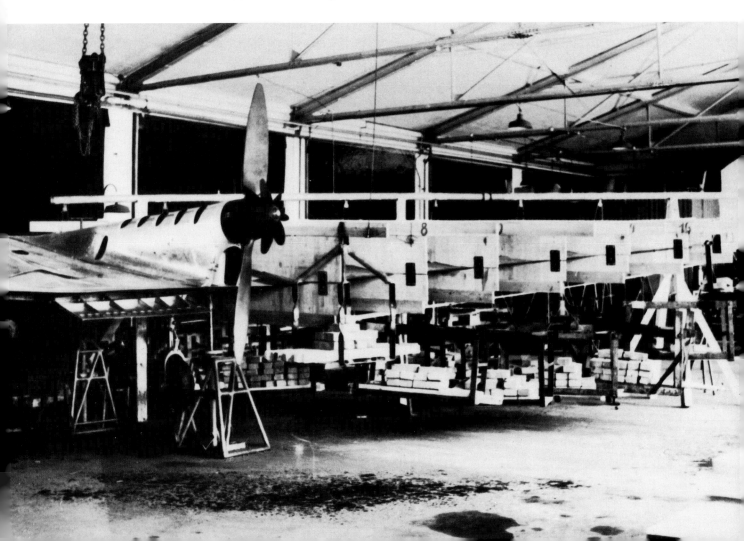

Walter Horten was a *Hauptmann* on the staff of Lln3. He managed to obtain a transfer to Göttingen, where he took over command of *Luftwaffenkommando IX*. Soon afterward, however, the *Kommando* was officially disbanded, and as a result Lln3 ceased to be the office responsible for development of the Horten projects. New life was injected into the Horten Firm, when, in August, Hermann Göring informed the company that work on the H IX turbojet fighter-bomber was to proceed with all urgency and that it was to construct a flyable, but unpowered, example as soon as possible.

*Luftwaffenkommando IX,* which officially no longer existed, continued to be funded and carried on its work, but without direct influence from the *Technischen Amt* of the RLM. The H IX V1 was an unpowered research glider and received the RLM-Number 8-229. The aircraft was of mixed construction (welded steel tube and wood) and was covered with several layers of plywood of various qualities, the outer layer being of the best quality. This method of construction made radar detection of the aircraft extremely difficult. The pilot was accommodated in a normal seated position. The first flight of the V1 took place on March 1, 1944, at Göttingen with Heinz Scheidhauer at the controls. Following several towed

Göttingen 1943/44: The H VII carries out its initial taxiing trials (the aircraft's retractable nosewheels, together with the wheel forks and shock absorbers, were taken from a wrecked Me 210). The military personnel in the photo are *Feldwebel* Knöpfle (left) and *Major* Walter Horten (right). The pilot is *Oberleutnant* Heinz Scheidhauer.
Following page: This view from below reveals some interesting details.

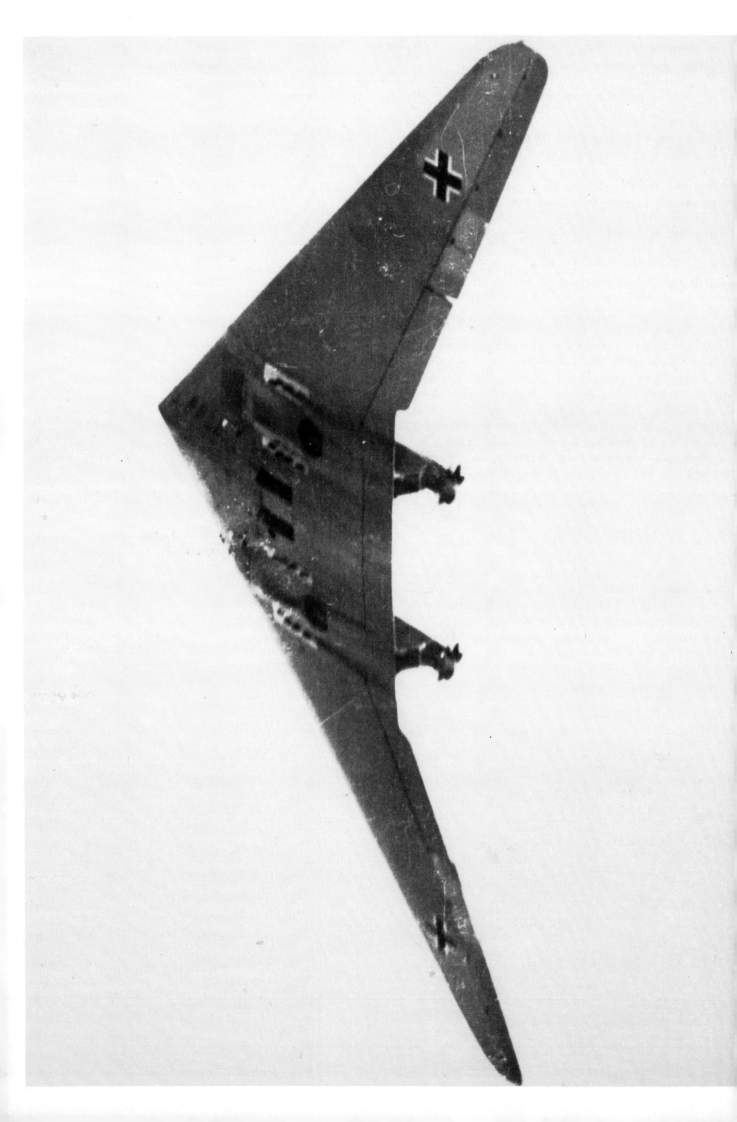

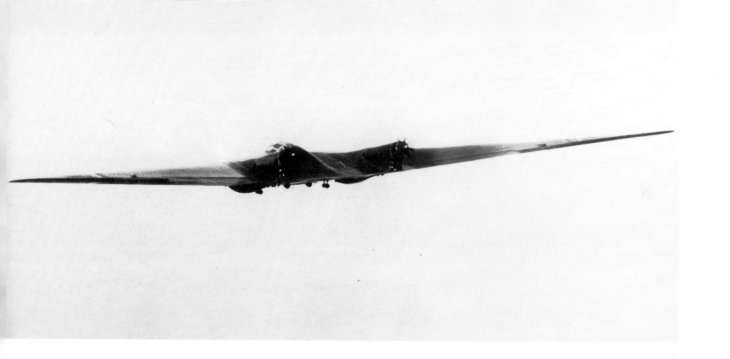

Various views of the H VII in flight and (below) in the hangar at Göttingen with extension shaft fairings removed.

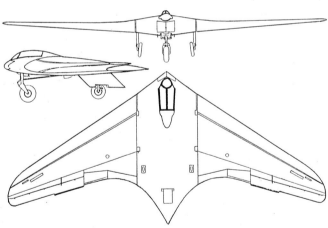

On the left is a three-view drawing of the H IX V1 research glider. In the photograph above the aircraft is seen under construction in the *Autobahnstrašenmeisterei* hangar in Göttingen.

takeoffs, the aircraft was sent to Oranienburg near Berlin for flight testing, with Scheidhauer as pilot. A brief report submitted by the DVL on April 7, 1944, indicated that the aircraft provided an excellent gun platform.

In order to simulate the stabilizing effect of the engines, which were absent from the V1, the aircraft's main undercarriage legs were faired from the outset; only the aircraft's nosewheel was retractable. On March 5 the nose gear failed after it developed a wobble on Oranienburg's concrete runway. A special pressure suit was to have replaced the absent cockpit pressurization, but was never used in practice.

The machine was sent to Brandis, where it was to be tested by the military and used for training purposes. It was found there by soldiers of the US 9th Armored Division at the end of the war and was later burned in a "clearing action."

### Horten H IX, Werk-Nr.39, 1944/45
The H IX V2 was a test machine powered by two Jumo 004 turbojets and was assigned the RLM number 8-229. It was the world's first turbojet-powered all-wing aircraft. The V2 had a fully retractable undercarriage and was unarmed. The pilot was accommodated in a conventional seated position.

The wings are loaded for transport to Göttingen airfield.

The center section of the H IX V1 at Göttingen before transport to the airfield. Visible in the photo above is the compartment for the aircraft's braking parachute.

The main undercarriage was not retractable and was fitted with streamlined fairings to compensate for the stabilizing effect of the missing power plants. The aircraft's retractable nosewheel was in fact the tailwheel from a wrecked He 177 heavy bomber.

WL - 445029

Above: The center section about to be transported to Göttingen airfield. Clearly visible are the two glazed panels on the underside of the aircraft. The photograph below shows the wings arriving at the airfield.

Serious difficulties and delays in construction arose when the planned BMW 003 engines had to be replaced by more powerful Jumo 004s. The diameter of the Junkers engine was greater than that of the BMW product, requiring redesign of the engine bays. Like its predecessors, the aircraft was of mixed construction. The V2's undercarriage consisted of the tailwheel from a wrecked He 177 bomber, which was used as nosewheel, and the main undercarriage from a Bf 109 fighter.

The first test flight was made from Oranienburg on February 2, 1945, with *Leutnant* Erwin Ziller at the controls, and lasted about 30 minutes. The Horten brothers had known Ziller from the competitions at the Wasserkuppe. Ziller had familiarized himself with all-wing aircraft in December 1944 and January 1945, making several flights in the Horten H IX V1 glider (an He 111 served as glider tug) and the twin-engined Horten H VII at Oranienburg.

The completed H IX V1 at Göttingen airfield, 1944. Below: Visible in this view from above is the outlined walkway for access to the aircraft's cockpit, also the braking parachute in its stowage compartment. Following page: A comparison with the H IIIe.

Ziller spent the last three days of December 1944 at *Erprobungsstelle Rechlin*, where he made a total of five flights in the Me 262. These flights provided Ziller with an opportunity to become familiar with the operation and characteristics of the Jumo 004 turbojet engine.

At the end of a second successful test flight on February 3, 1945, Ziller deployed the aircraft's braking parachute too soon on his landing approach. The result was a hard landing which damaged the aircraft's main undercarriage. Con-

sequently, the third test flight in the Horten H IX did not take place until February 18, 1945. Returning after about 45 minutes in the air, Ziller was seen to dive the aircraft and pull up several times at an altitude of about 800 meters, apparently in an effort to relight an engine. The undercarriage was lowered unusually early, at an altitude of about 400 meters. The V2's speed decreased and, accompanied by increasing engine noise, its nose dropped and the aircraft entered a right-hand turn. The H IX completed a 360 degree turn with

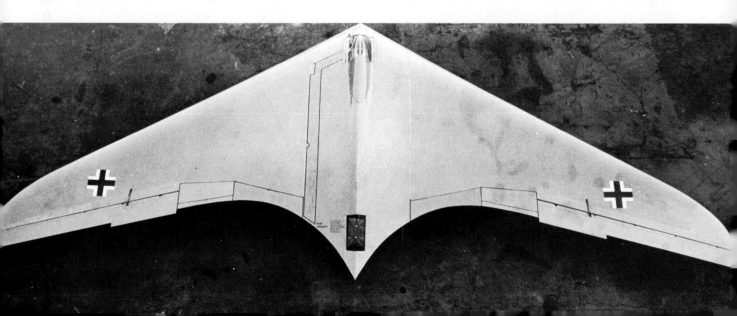

Previous page: The H IX V1 seen with its elevons and flaps in various positions. This page: The aircraft at Göttingen airfield.

The H IX V1 in flight; the pilot is Heinz Scheidhauer (below left). In the photo, below right, the aircraft is pictured being prepared for takeoff.

Above left: Heinz Scheidhauer climbs into the aircraft, and the signal is given for the He 111 glider tug to begin its takeoff. Below: After a flight — the braking parachute has been rolled up loosely and placed on the aft section of the aircraft.

its wings banked 20 degrees. It then accelerated and completed a second and third 360 degree turn, the angle of bank increasing all the while. As it began a fourth circle, the aircraft struck the frozen turf beyond the airfield boundary.

Walter Rösler was the first Horten employee to reach the crash site, about two-and-a-half minutes after the accident. In his report he stated: "The first thing I saw was the two Junkers engines lying on the other side of the embankment. I could hear the turbine running down in the still-warm left power plant, while there was not a sound from the cooled-off right engine which lay beside it. . ." There was a strong smell of fuel, but no fire. Other than the jet engines and plexiglass cockpit hood, the aircraft had been completely destroyed. Like the engines, Ziller was ejected from the aircraft on impact. He was thrown against a large tree and killed instantly. Ziller had not used his radio, and had continued to fly the aircraft with an engine out and the undercarriage extended. He did not

Above left: Roll-out on February 28, 1944; on the right is the retractable nosewheel. Below: The H IX V1 lying on its nose after pilot Scheidhauer retracted the nosewheel to act as an "emergency brake." The airfield at Göttingen proved too short.

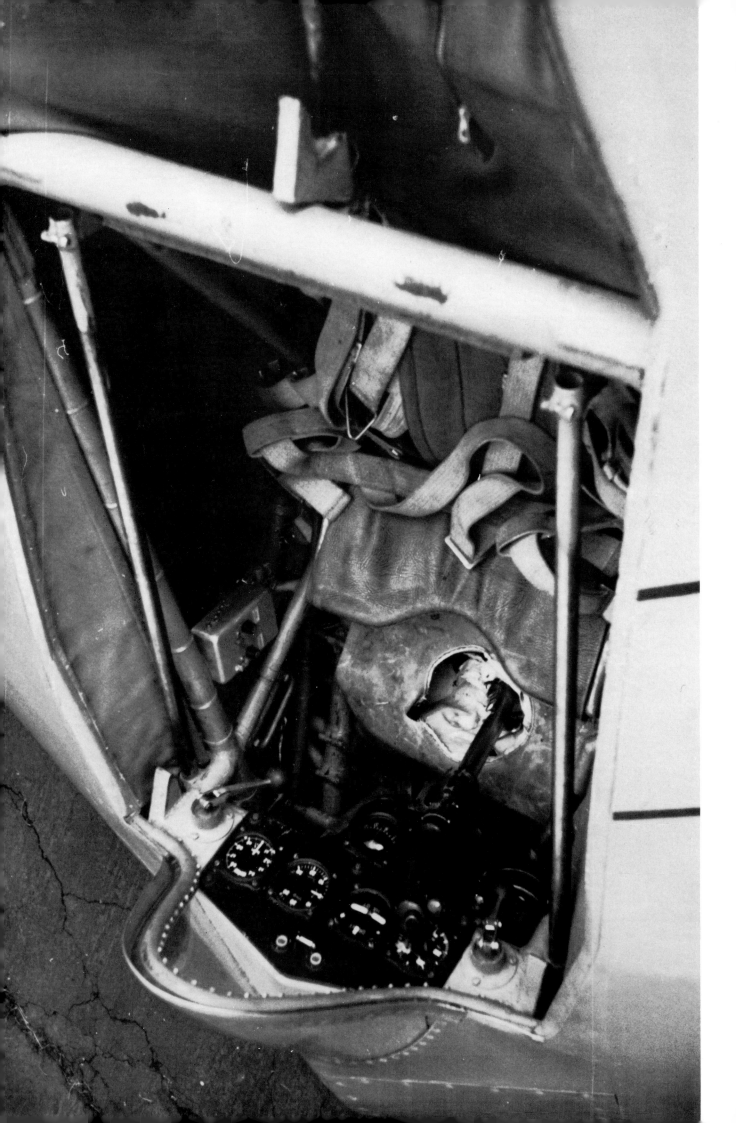

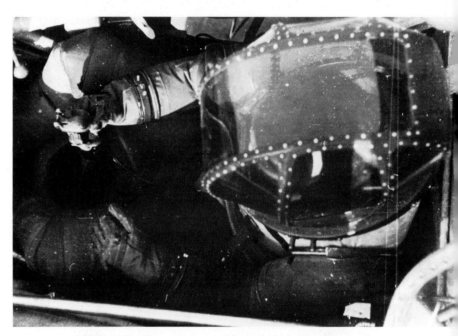

Facing page: A view of the aircraft's instrument panel, from left to right: turn and bank indicator, altimeter, vertical speed indicator (variometer), airspeed indicator and below it the compass.

This page: A pressure suit was to have to have taken the place of cockpit pressurization, but was not used in practice.

Following page: The H IX V1 as found by US troops at Brandis.

Subsequent page: An RLM specification sheet depicting the original design.

attempt to use his ejection seat and parachute to safety, and the aircraft's canopy was not jettisoned. It seems certain that he was attempting to save the valuable aircraft.

What had happened? The empty compressed air bottle in the wreckage confirmed that the under-carriage had been lowered with compressed air after a loss of hydraulic power following the failure of an engine. Had there been a stall, beginning at the right wingtip? Had the test pilot been rendered unconscious and unable to react by carbonizing oil from the remaining engine, which had eventually overheated? (There were no bulk-heads separating the cockpit from the engine bays.)

Unfortunately, only *Leutnant* Ziller could have answered these questions, and he had failed to survive. In the opinion of the investigating experts sabotage could not be ruled out.

### Horten H IX V3, RLM-Number 8-229
The H IX V3 was an unarmed, twin-jet, single-seat aircraft. Further production of the fighter-bomber was assigned to the Gothaer Waggon-fabrik (GWF). Well-known for its Go 241 cargo

glider, Gotha was considered the company best suited to manufacture Horten aircraft. The air-craft's turbojet engines were installed splayed 15 degrees left and right of the aircraft centerline and 4 degrees nose down. The new installation was tested in a center section mock-up. Construction of the H IX V3 was nearly complete when the Gotha Works at Friederichsroda was overrun by troops of the American 3rd Army's VII Corps on April 14, 1945. The aircraft was assigned the number T2-490 by the Americans. The aircraft's official RLM designation is uncertain, as it was referred to as the Ho 229 as well as the Go 229. Also found in the destroyed and abandoned works were several other prototypes in various stages of con-struction, including a two-seat version.

The V3 was sent to the United States by ship, along with other captured aircraft, and finally ended up in the H. H. "Hap" Arnold collection of the Air Force Technical Museum. The all-wing aircraft was to have been brought to flying status at Park Ridge, Illinois, but budget cuts in the late forties and early fifties brought these plans to an end. The V3 was handed over to the present-day National Air and Space Museum (NASM) in Washington D.C.

| RLM | Flugzeugtypenblatt | Baumuster: „Horten IX" |
|---|---|---|
| | | Bauausführg.: V1, V2. |
| | | Baureihe: |

Bildskizze | Maßstab 1:100 | Maße in mm

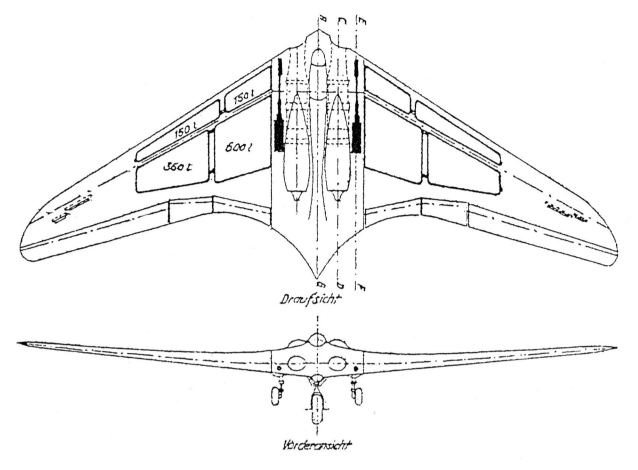

150 l
150 l
600 l
360 l

Draufsicht

Vorderansicht

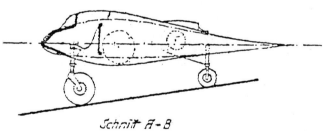

Schnitt A-B

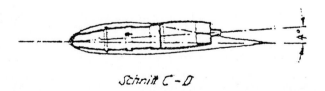

4°

Schnitt C-D

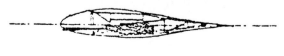

Schnitt E-F

39

The men of the *Strassenmeisterei Göttingen* before the steel tube center section of the H IX V2 (see also below). On the left is the rebuilt H II D - 10 -125, modified as a flying test-bed for the H IX. Right, a three-view drawing of the V2.

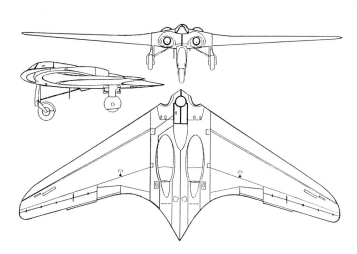

The V2's nosewheel was in fact a tailwheel from a wrecked He 177, including retraction cylinder and hydraulics. The parts were provided by the Göttingen salvage organization. Right: The Jumo 004-B turbojet, which powered the H IX V2; below is the BMW 003, which was originally chosen. Below left: Moving the wings "by hand."

The first all-wing fighter-bomber, the H IX V2, under construction.

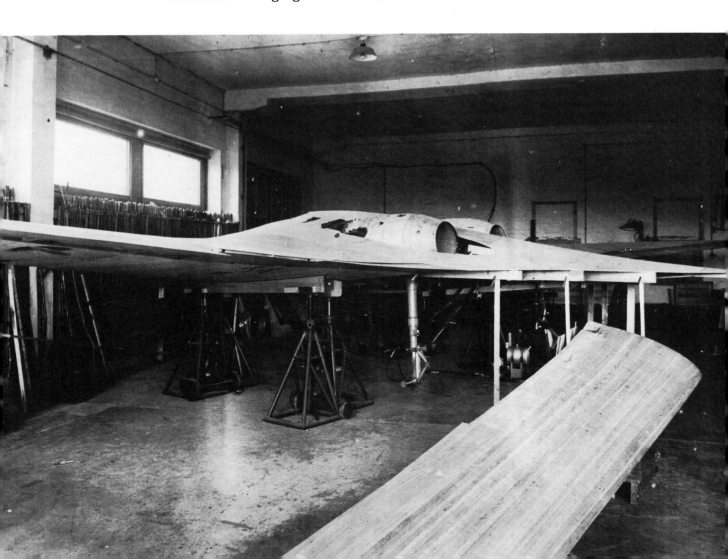

Assembly took place in a three-car garage.

The H IX V2 is prepared for takeoff on the runway at Oranienburg, February 1945.

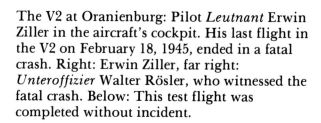

The V2 at Oranienburg: Pilot *Leutnant* Erwin Ziller in the aircraft's cockpit. His last flight in the V2 on February 18, 1945, ended in a fatal crash. Right: Erwin Ziller, far right: *Unteroffizier* Walter Rösler, who witnessed the fatal crash. Below: This test flight was completed without incident.

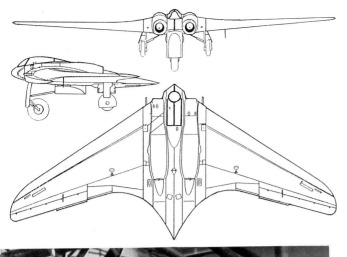

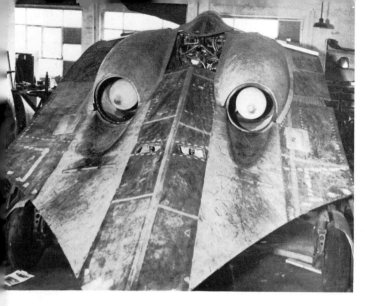

Facing page: Three-view drawing of the H IX V3, now also known as the Ho 229. Later, after production had been assigned to the Gotha Firm, it was also designated Go 229. The drawing does not represent the aircraft actually built, which had a slightly different flap arrangement. The engine installation was tested in a mock-up. This page: The Ho 220 V3 following its capture by US forces.

The center section in the USA, and finally in storage in the annex of the National Air and Space Museum, Silver Hill, Maryland, where the aircraft still resides today.

Below: The Ho 229's speed brake, seen in the extended position.

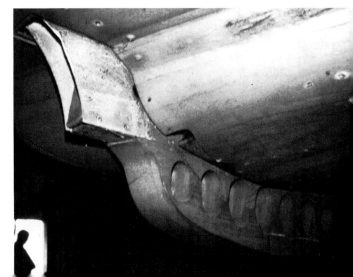

The aircraft at Silver Hill. Below: The cockpit with a view of the instrument panel. From left to right: Undercarriage control panel, ignition switches, vertical speed indicator, turn and bank indicator, airspeed indicator, fuel warning light; 2nd row: flap control panel, altimeter (removed), master repeater compass, clock, two fuel indicators; 3rd row: injection pressure indicator (left), gas temperature indicator (left), RPM indicators (left and right), gas temperature indicator (right), injection pressure indicator (right), outside temperature indicator; below, oxygen valves.

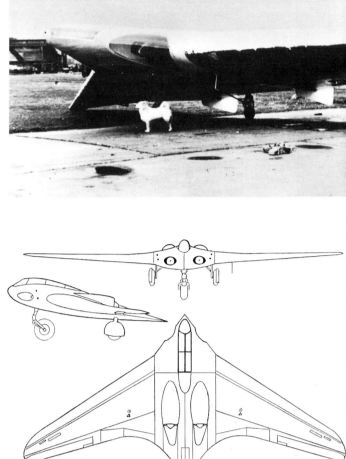

Sketch of the planned two-seat Ho 229 V6 and the H II modified as a flying test-bed with extended nose.

When US troops arrived they found the V6 under construction.

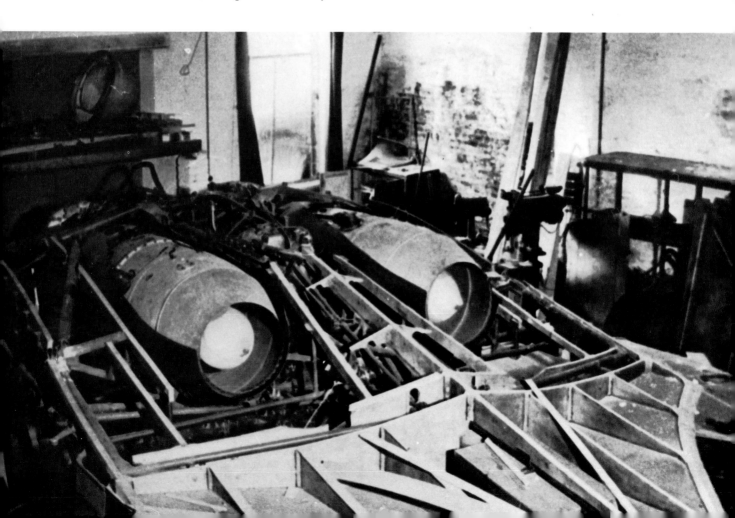

# Technical Data

| Type | Span/m | Length/m | Height/m | Empty weight/kg | Gross weight/kg | Power plants | Output | Maximum speed/kph | Cruise speed/kph | Landing speed/kph | Crew | Armament | Remarks |
|---|---|---|---|---|---|---|---|---|---|---|---|---|---|
| Horten H Va | 14.00 | – | – | 1,600 | 1,840 | 2xHirth HM60R | 80 HP each | 280 | 250 | 84 | 2 in prone position | – | Research aircraft, synthetic materials |
| Horten Vb | 16.00 | 6.00 | 2.10 | 1,360 | 1,600 | 2xHirth HM60R | 80 HP each | 260 | 230 | 70 | 2 in prone position | – | research aircraft, mixed wood and steel tube construction |
| Horten Vc | 16.00 | 6.00 | – | 1,440 | 1,600 | 2xHirth HM60R | 80 HP each | 260 | 230 | 70 | 1 seated | – | Research aircraft, mixed wood and steel tube construction |
| Horten H VII | 16.00 | 7.40 | 2.60 | 2,200 | 3,200 | 2xArgus AS10C | 240 HP each | 340 | 310 | 100 | 2 seated | – | Fighter trainer Ho 226, wood-Dural construction |
| Horten IX V1 | 16.76 | 7.60 | – | 1,900 | 2,000 | – | – | – | – | 75 | 1 | – | Research aircraft, wood and steel tube construction |
| Horten H IX V2 | 16.76 | 7.47 | 2.81 | 4,844 | 6,876 | 2xJumo 004B-2 | 900 kg each | 977 | 690 | 145 | 1 seated | – | Fighter test aircraft, wood and steel tube construction |
| Horten H IX V3 | 16.80 | 7.47 | 2.81 | 5,067 | 8,999 | 2xJumo 004B-2 | 900 kg each | 977 | 632 | 156 | 1 seated | 2xMK 103 or 4xMK 108 or 2xMK 108 and 2xRB8-/81 | Fighter-bomber Ho Prototype Reconnaissance Aircraft |
| Horten H IX V4 | | | | | | | | | | | 1 seated | | Ho229 B-1 night fighter |
| Horten H IX V5 | | | | | | | | | | | 1 seated | | Ho 229 B-1 night fighter |
| Horten H IX V6 | 16.76 | | | | | 2xJumo 004B-2 | 900 kg each | | | | 2 seated | | Trainer, night fighter trainer |
| Horten IX V7 | 16.76 | | | | | 2xJumo 004B-2 | 900 kg each | | | | 2 seated | 4xMK 108 or 2xMK 103 | Prototype 3. A-Series with full equipment |
| Horten IX V8 | | | | | | | | | | | | | *1000 kg bomb load |

Above: The H XVIII project reached far into the future: a six-engined, turbojet-powered, long-range bomber. The project was given to the Horten brothers by Hermann Göring on March 12, 1945.

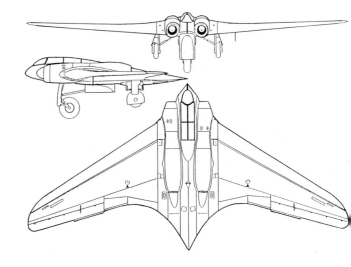

The steel tube center section was very probably the initial construction phase of this aircraft.

Three-view drawing of the V7.